*for Benita Valente, soprano, Cynthia Raim, piano
and Donald Hall
in memory of Jane Kenyon*

William Bolcom

Briefly It Enters

a cycle of songs from poems of Jane Kenyon

for voice and piano

This project is supported in part by a grant from the National Endowment for the Arts and was commissioned by the University Musical Society of the University of Michigan, San Francisco Performances, the University of Wisconsin-Madison, Dartmouth College Hopkins Center and the University of New Hampshire Celebrity Series.

ISBN 0-7935-9132-5

EXCLUSIVELY DISTRIBUTED BY

HAL•LEONARD® CORPORATION

7777 W. BLUEMOUND RD. P.O. BOX 13819 MILWAUKEE, WI 53213

Jane Kenyon's passion for music was as great as her genius for writing poetry. Before we left Michigan in 1975, we came to know William Bolcom and Joan Morris, who visited us several times on our farm in New Hampshire. When Jane contracted leukemia in 1994, Bill had already set Jane's "Let Evening Come" in a cantata.

While she was ill she listened over and over again, with the greatest pleasure, to a tape of Benita Valente singing her words.

She loved Bill's music and Benita Valente's voice. Bill was already planning "Briefly It Enters," for Benita Valente, which was a thrill for Jane to imagine. She corresponded with Bill about the choice of poems before she died at forty-seven on 22 April 1995.

– Donald Hall

ACKNOWLEDGEMENT

"Who", "The Clearing", "Otherwise", "February: Thinking of Flowers", "Twilight: After Haying", "Man Eating", "The Sick Wife", "Peonies at Dusk", "Briefly It Enters, and Briefly Speaks" copyright © 1996 by the Estate of Jane Kenyon. Reproduced from *Otherwise: New & Selected Poems* with the permission of Graywolf Press, Saint Paul, Minnesota.

CONTENTS

1. Who

Jane Kenyon

William Bolcom

pans.... Who is it who asks me to find lan-guage for the

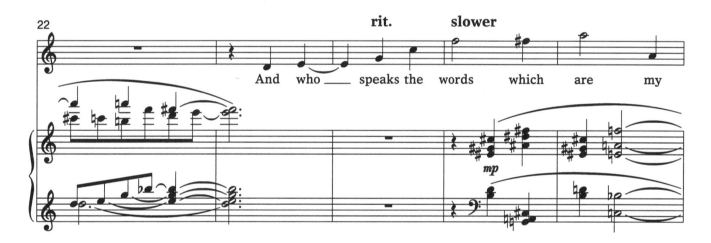

sound _____ a sheep's hoof makes when it strikes a stone? _____

And who ___ speaks the words which are my

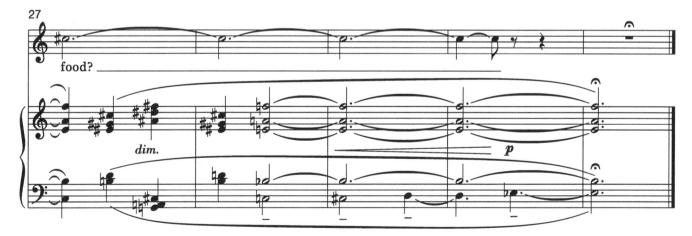

food? _____

2. The Clearing

Dancelike, spirited, a little bumptious ♩ = 144

The dog and I push through the ring of drip-ping ju-ni-pers

to en-ter the o - pen space high on the hill where I let him off the

leash.   He vaults, snuf-fling, be-tween tufts of

moss;   twigs snap be-neath his weight; he rolls and rubs his

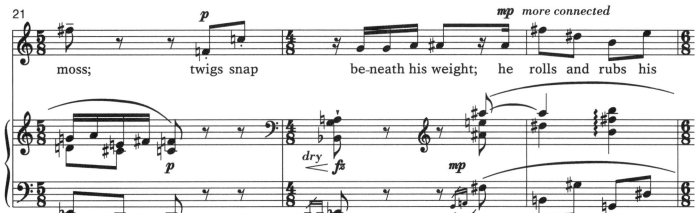

jowls on the ar-o-mat-ic earth;   his pink tongue

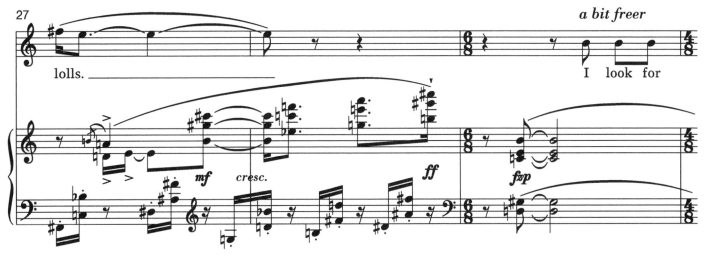

lolls.   I look for

sticks of prop - er heft to throw for him, while he sits, prim and ear-nest

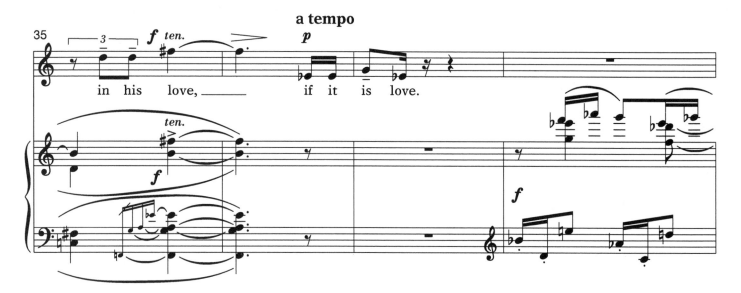

in his love, _____ if it is love.

Much slower (Tempo II) ♩ = c. 50

All night a soak-ing rain, — and now the hill __

with much 𝄐.

ex-hales re-lief, and the fra-grance of warm earth . . . .

tratt.

Tempo I

The sedg-es have grown an inch since yes-ter-day, and _

ferns un - furled, and e-ven if they try __ the li-lacs by the

barn can't keep from o-pen-ing to - day.

Tempo II

I longed for spring's thou-sand ten-der greens, _

Tempo I

poco rit.

_____ and the white-throat-ed spar-row's call _____ that bor-ders on

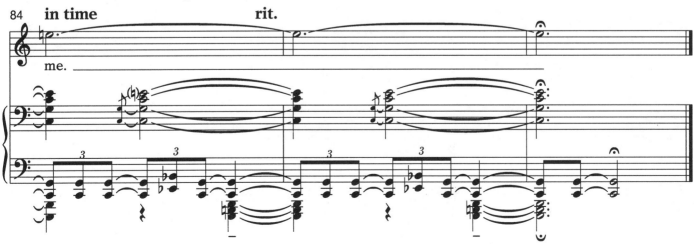

3. Otherwise

birch wood.— All— morn-ing I did the work I love.

At noon I lay down with my— mate.— It might have been

oth-er-wise.——— We ate din-ner to-geth-er at a ta - ble— with sil-ver

can-dle-sticks. It might have been oth-er-wise.——— I

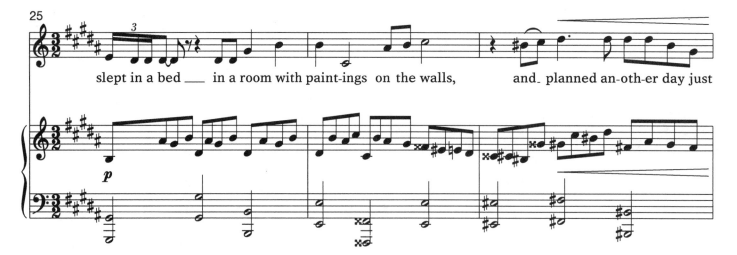

slept in a bed ___ in a room with paint-ings on the walls, and. planned an-oth-er day just

like this day. ___ But one day, I know, _____ it will be

oth-er-wise. _____

4. February: Thinking of Flowers

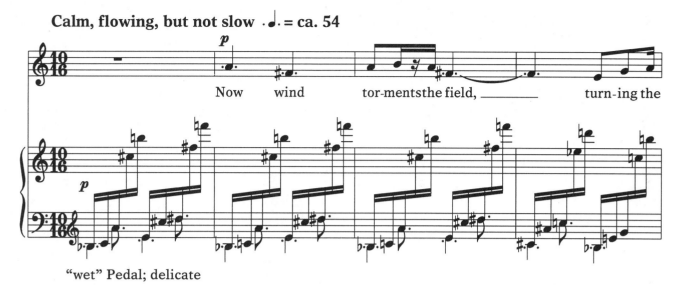

Calm, flowing, but not slow ♩. = ca. 54

p

Now wind tor-ments the field, _____ turn-ing the

"wet" Pedal; delicate

white sur-face back on it - self, back and back on it - self, like an

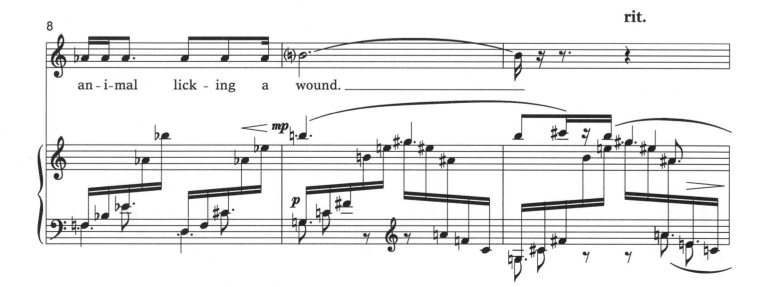

an - i - mal lick - ing a wound. _____

rit.

Noth-ing but white— the air, the light; on - ly one brown_

_ milk - weed pod bob-bing in the gul-ly, small - est brown boat on the im-

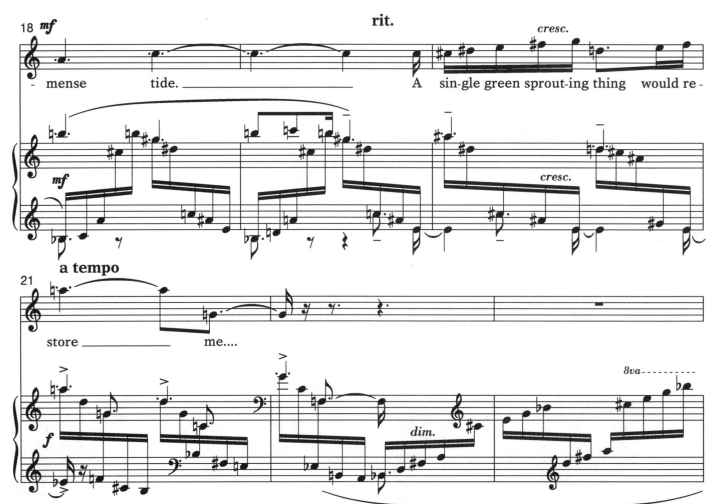

- mense tide. _____ A sin-gle green sprout-ing thing would re-

store _____ me....

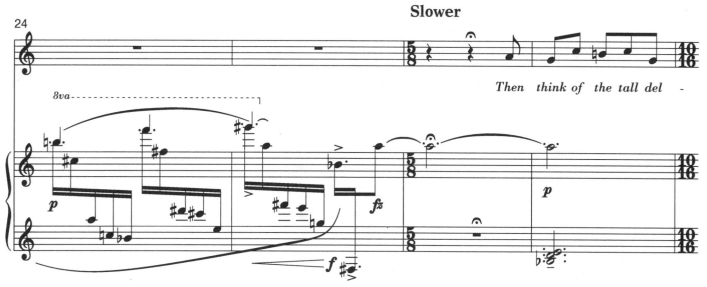

Then think of the tall del -

phi-ni-um, sway-ing, or the bee

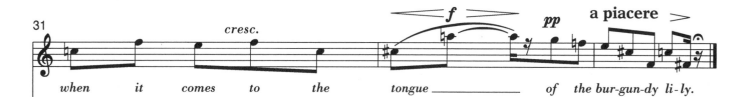

when it comes to the tongue _____ of the bur-gun-dy li-ly.

for J.V.
in memoriam Jane Kenyon

5. Twilight: After Haying

Stately ♩ = 80 **(in 1)**

Yes,_____ long

shad-ows go out from the bales; and____ yes,_____ the soul__ must

part from the bod-y;_____ what else could it do?

The men sprawl____ near the bal - er, too____ tired to leave the field.____

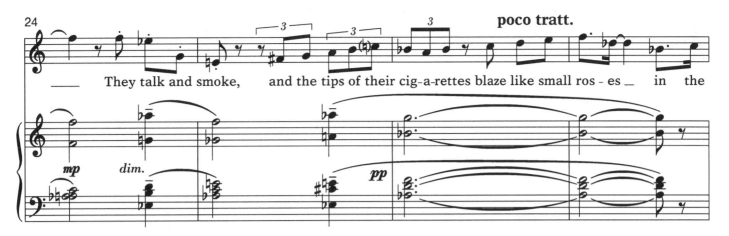

They talk and smoke, and the tips of their cig-a-rettes blaze like small ros - es _ in the

night air. _____ (It ar - rived and set-tled a-mong them be-fore they_ were a-

- ware.) _____ The moon comes to count the bales, _____ and the

dis-pos-sessed— _ Whip-poor-will, _____ Whip-poor-will _____ —sings from the dust-y

stub-ble.

These things hap-pen .... the soul's bliss and

freely

suf-fer-ing are bound to-geth-er like the grass-es ....

as before

The last, sweet ex-hal-a-tions

of tim - o - thy and vetch go out ___ with the song ___ of ___ the bird; ___

Very slow

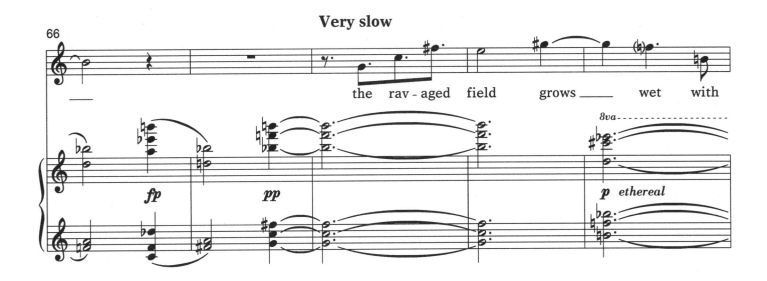

the rav - aged field grows ___ wet with

rit.   *lunga*

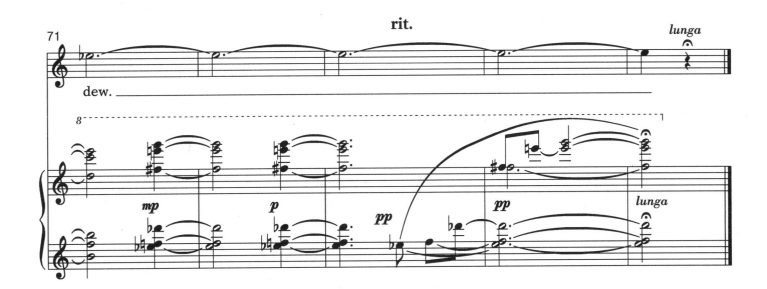

dew. ___

6. Man Eating

The man at the ta-ble a-cross from mine is eat - ing yo-gurt. His eyes, fol-low-ing the pro-gress of the spoon, cross brief - ly each time it nears his face.

Time, _____ and the world with all its prin-ci - pa-li - ties, _____

23

7. The Sick Wife

day _____ and so on - ly mo-thers with small child-ren or re-tired cou-ples

(r.h. sempre pp)

(sempre u.c.) p

8ba- - - - - - - - - - - - - - -

stepped through the mud - dy park-ing lot. __

mp

8ba- -

Dry clean - ing swung _____ and

mp

mf

8ba- - - - - - - - - - - - - - - - - -

gleamed on hang-ers in the cars of the pros-per-ous. How

p

mf

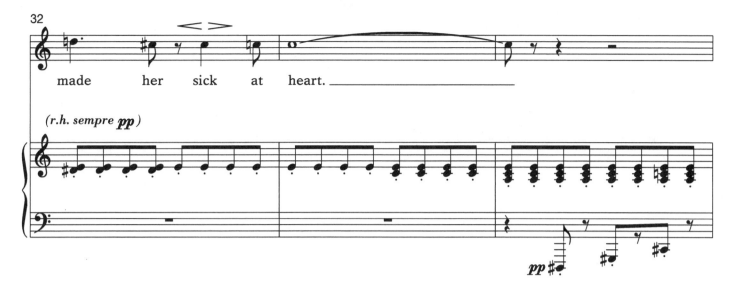

made her sick at heart._____

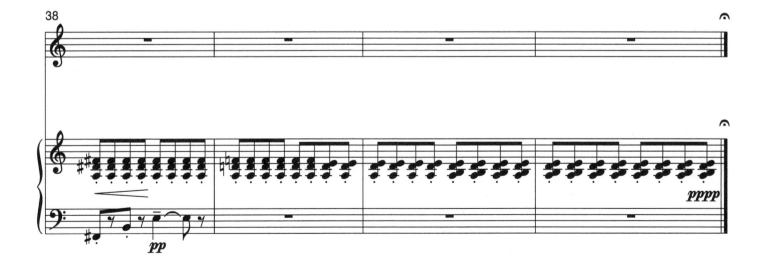

8. Peonies at Dusk

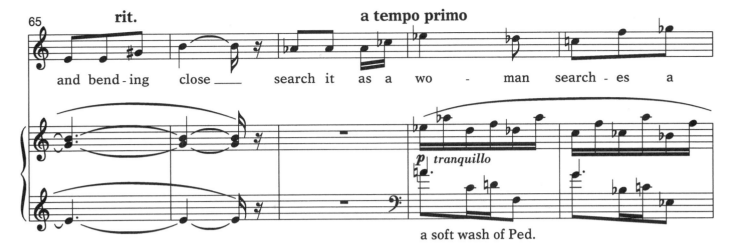

9. Briefly It Enters, and Briefly Speaks

Stately (♩ = 66) but not dragging; ecstatic

f rich and warm

dim.   *p*

I am the blos - som _ pressed _ in a book, found a-

gain ___ af - ter two hun - dred years.... I am the mak - er the lov - er, and the

keep - er.... *mf* *f* *mf* When the young girl _ who starves

mp *mp*

* *until* in original; variant approved by poet Donald Hall, Kenyon's widower.

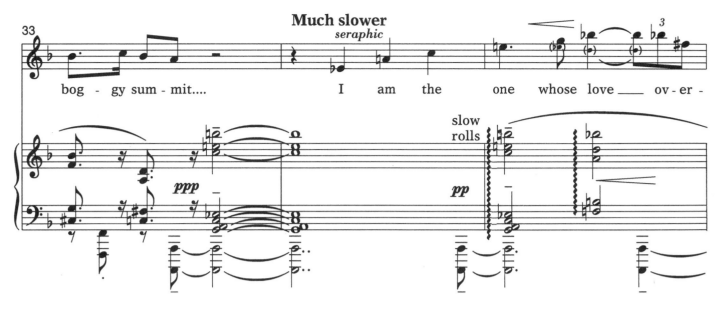

bog - gy sum - mit.... I am the one whose love __ ov - er -

comes you, al - read - y with you _____ when you think to call my

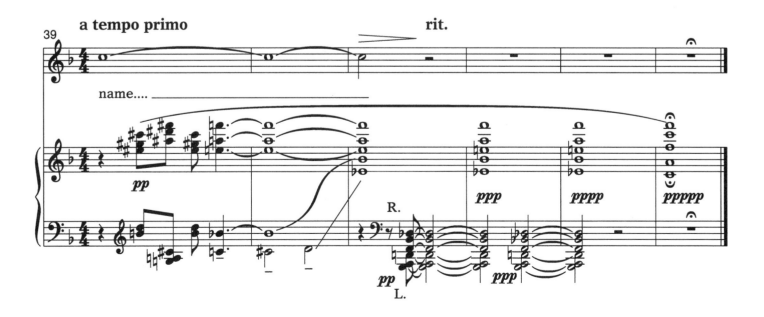

name.... _____